The
Lincoln
Memorial

A Great President Remembered

The Lincoln Memorial

A Great President Remembered

Frederic Gilmore

THE CHILD'S WORLD®, INC.

Library of Congress Cataloging-in-Publication Data
Gilmore, Frederic.
The Lincoln Memorial : a great president remembered / by Frederic Gilmore.
p.   cm.
Includes index.
Summary: Describes the history of the Lincoln Memorial,
how it was built, and what it represents.
ISBN 1-56766-759-7
1. Lincoln Memorial (Washington, D.C.)—Juvenile literature.
2. Lincoln, Abraham, 1809-1865—Monuments—Washington (D.C.)—Juvenile literature.
3. Washington (D.C.)—Buildings, structures, etc.—Juvenile literature.
[1. Lincoln Memorial (Washington, D.C.) 2. National monuments.]   I. Title.
F203.4.L73 G55   2000
975.3—dc21   99-086280

Credits

© Archive Photos: 29
© Bruce Jackson/Gnass Photo Images: cover, 30
© Bruce Leighty/The Image Finders: 15
© Chris Cheadle/Tony Stone Worldwide: 24
© Chuck Pefley/Tony Stone Images: 2
© Frederic Lewis/Archive Photos: 19
© Glen Allison/Tony Stone Images: 23
© Hulton Getty: 6, 9
© Mark S. Skalny/Visuals Unlimited: 16
© National Archives (115-JD-315): 13
© Parks & History Association: 20
© UPI/Corbis-Bettman: 10
© William B. Folsom: 26

On the cover...

Front cover: The statue of Abraham Lincoln glows softly at night in the Lincoln Memorial.
Page 2: Lincoln's statue looks out past the columns of the memorial at sunset.

Table of Contents

On April 14, 1865, the president of the United States, Abraham Lincoln, went to a play at Ford's Theater in Washington, D.C. While President Lincoln and his wife watched the play, a man named John Wilkes Booth approached Lincoln from behind. Booth pointed a gun at President Lincoln and shot him in the back of the head. Booth then ran from the theater. While Booth made his escape, President Lincoln lay dying. He died the next day.

John Booth killed the 16th president of the United States. He killed the man who had freed the slaves. He killed the man who had gone to war to save the Union we call the United States. People around the world were shocked. The people of the United States were in **mourning.** The leader of the United States was dead.

⇐ **This drawing shows John Wilkes Booth firing the shot that killed President Lincoln.**

After Abraham Lincoln's death, many people across the United States thought that it was important to remember him. They wanted to remember Lincoln's actions as well as the **virtues** that he believed were important. Different groups of people had different ideas about how best to remember and show respect for Lincoln's achievements. However, these groups could not come to an agreement.

Thousands of people lined the streets of Washington, ⇒ D.C. to watch Lincoln's funeral procession.

On February 19, 1911, the United States Congress created the *Lincoln Memorial Commission*. This group of people was to select a site and present a plan for a monument to honor Lincoln. The commission chose a location in Washington, D.C., called Potomac Park for the memorial. This site had a good view of the White House, the Washington Monument, and the Capitol building. The commission asked architects to draw ideas for the memorial. Henry Bacon was an architect in New York. Bacon gave the commission a plan for a memorial building. His idea was presented to Congress and approved.

Workers began preparing the site for the memorial on February 12, 1914. The date was important because it was the 105th anniversary of Abraham Lincoln's birth.

The location chosen for the new memorial building was swampy and wet. The workers had to build a platform strong enough to support the weight of the building. The platform was 14 feet high, 257 feet long, and 187 feet wide—almost as big as a football field. Dirt was put around the platform to form a mound. After a year of work on the platform base, the first stone of the memorial building was set in place on February 12, 1915.

This photo shows the site of the memorial before it ⇒ was built. You can see the Capitol in the distance.

Henry Bacon's plans for the memorial building were modeled after very old Greek architecture. **Marble** was used to build most of the memorial. Marble is very hard and lasts a long time, even when exposed to rain and snow. The memorial building has a huge marble roof supported by large marble columns. The columns are 44 feet high and more than 7 feet across. Thirty-six columns support the roof. That was the number of states in the Union when Lincoln was president. Lincoln fought the Civil War to keep the 36 states united as one country.

It is easier to see the columns and ⇒ huge roof from farther away.

Different kinds of marble as well as other hard stones were used to construct the memorial. These stones were brought from many different states. The floor of the memorial is made of Tennessee Pink marble. The columns and the outside of the building are Colorado Yule marble. The walls inside the memorial are Indiana limestone. The ceiling is made from **translucent** Alabama marble. When the memorial building was completed, it was as tall as a nine-story building.

⇐ **This photo of the memorial's ceiling shows the different types of marble.**

Bacon's plan also called for a statue of Lincoln to be placed in the center of the building near the back. But Bacon was an architect, not an artist.

To build the statue of Lincoln, the Memorial Commission chose Daniel Chester French. French was an American **sculptor** who had studied art in Paris, France. He was considered to be the best American sculptor at the time. The Lincoln Memorial Commission asked French to sculpt a statue of Lincoln that would be at least 10 feet tall. Bacon and French decided that a statue of Lincoln sitting down would best represent the difficult times the former president endured.

French made a small model of the statue and showed it to the commission. The members of the commission approved the idea for the statue on February 28, 1916.

Daniel Chester French, the sculptor who carved Lincoln's statue. ⇒

To create a realistic and lifelike statue of the president, French used photographs and a "life mask" of Lincoln. The life mask was actually a plaster mold of the president's face that was made back when Lincoln was alive. The mask was created by an artist named Leonard Volk, who met with Lincoln in 1860 when Lincoln was a **candidate** for the presidency. Volk wrote down detailed measurements of Lincoln's upper body. He made plaster molds of Lincoln's hands, too.

French used Volk's measurements of Lincoln, the life mask, and the plaster casts of Lincoln's hands to make his statue as lifelike as possible.

French made plans to begin the final statue of Lincoln that would be the centerpiece of the memorial. At the same time, work on the memorial building slowed in 1917 because the United States had entered World War I. Bacon saw one of French's models of the statue and began to think it was too small for the large memorial building. After comparing photographs of the building and the model of the statue, Bacon and French decided that the statue would have to be much larger than the 10-foot height they had planned.

Bacon and French asked the Lincoln Memorial Commission for permission to make the statue of Lincoln 19 feet tall. The commission approved the request.

From close up, it is easy to see how carefully ⇒ French carved Lincoln's statue.

After getting approval for the larger statue, French made another model. He then started the plans for the statue. French needed help for a statue this big. He hired the Piccirilli brothers to cut the marble stone. The Piccirilli brothers were well known for their work in stonecutting. The statue would be carved out of Georgia White marble. But French could not find a big enough piece of marble without any flaws. French would need to put the statue of Lincoln together from pieces of marble.

With French's model as their guide, the Piccirilli brothers and French carved the huge statue of Lincoln out of 28 pieces of perfect marble. They then placed the pieces together to form the statue. Like pieces of a puzzle, the statue of Lincoln began to take shape in the memorial building. In May of 1920 the statue of Lincoln was finished and the memorial building was nearing completion.

⇐ **French even put lots of details into Lincoln's clothes.**

An artist named Jules Guerin was hired to paint two **murals** on the walls inside the memorial. The murals are 60 feet long and 12 feet high. One of the murals shows the **emancipation** of slaves. The other shows the unity of the northern and southern states. Also inside the memorial, two famous speeches by Lincoln are carved into the walls.

Lights were added to allow people to view the memorial at night. In the following year, trees and grass were planted around the memorial.

⇐ **This is the north mural, "Unification." Here the Angel of Truth joins the hands of the North and South.**   **27**

The Lincoln Memorial was dedicated during a ceremony on Memorial Day, May 30, 1922. The Chief Justice of the Supreme Court, William Howard Taft, presented the memorial to the president of the United States, Warren G. Harding. In front of 50,000 people, President Harding accepted the memorial on behalf of the American people. The guest of honor at the dedication ceremony was Robert Todd Lincoln, the only living son of former President Lincoln.

Since the dedication ceremony, many events have occurred at the Lincoln Memorial. The most famous may have been a speech by Dr. Martin Luther King, Jr., on August 28, 1963. From the steps of the Lincoln Memorial, King gave a speech called "I Have a Dream." More than 200,000 people were at the Lincoln Memorial that day to hear him speak.

This picture shows Martin Luther King, Jr., ⇒ speaking to the crowd on August 28, 1963.

Today you can visit the Lincoln Memorial if you go to Washington, D.C. The memorial is located at the west end of a large reflecting pool. At the other end of the pool is the Washington Monument, and behind that is the Capitol dome. If you cannot get to Washington, D.C., you can see a picture of the Lincoln Memorial if you look on the back side of a penny. If you look very closely, you can even see French's statue of Lincoln sitting in the middle of the memorial building.

⇐ **The Lincoln Memorial glows
in the light just after sunset.**

Glossary

candidate (KAN–dih–dayt)
A candidate is a person who is running in an election. Abraham Lincoln was a candidate for the presidency in 1860 when his life mask was created.

emancipation (ee–man–sih–PAY–shun)
Emancipation is the act of freeing someone from the control of something or someone else. Lincoln was responsible for emancipating slaves in the United States.

marble (MAR–bull)
Marble is a type of stone that is very hard and good for building. Many different types of marble were used in the Lincoln Memorial.

mourning (MOR–ning)
Mourning is showing sadness for a person's death. The American people were in mourning after President Lincoln was killed.

murals (MYOOR–ullz)
A mural is artwork that is made to be an important part of a wall or ceiling. There are two murals inside the Lincoln Memorial.

sculptor (SKULP–ter)
A sculptor is a person who makes artwork out of solid objects. Daniel Chester French was the sculptor who made the statue of President Lincoln.

translucent (tranz–LOO–sent)
An object that you cannot see through—but that some light can still pass through—is called translucent. A translucent type of marble was used in the ceiling of the Lincoln Memorial.

virtues (VIR–chooz)
A personal quality or trait that people see as being good is called a virtue. President Lincoln had many virtues.

Index

Web Sites

Learn more about the Lincoln Memorial:
http://www.nps.gov/linc/index2.htm

Learn more about Abraham Lincoln:
http://members.aol.com/RVSNorton/Lincoln2.html

http://www.historyplace.com/lincoln/index.html